It Is Fun To Read

Book One
Revised Edition

Christian Liberty Press
Arlington Heights, Illinois 60004

A publication of
Christian Liberty Press
502 West Euclid Avenue
Arlington Heights, Illinois 60004
www.christianlibertypress.com

IT IS FUN TO READ
    1. Phonics—Juvenile literature
    2. Reading—Juvenile literature
Written by
    Florence M. Lindstrom
Copyediting by
    Belit M. Shewan
    Edward J. Shewan
Cover Design by
    Eric D. Bristley

Illustrations by
    Vic Lockman
Colorization of Illustrations by
    Christopher D. Kou
Graphics and layout by
    Eric D. Bristley
    Christopher D. Kou
    Edward J. Shewan

ISBN 1-930092-27-X

Printed in the United States of America

Contents

Lesson 1

A a

ant

| Jăn | Dăn | Dăd |
| Jan | Dan | Dad |

can	Dan	Jan
Jan	Jan	ran
Dan	ran	Dad

| ănd | ăs | and |
| and | fast | fast |

sēē

see   Dad can see Dan and Jan.

Dan and Jan

Dan ran.
Jan ran.
Dan ran fast.
Jan ran as fast as Dan.
Dad can see Dan and Jan.

Lesson 2

A a

ant

hănd	ăm	băg
hand	am	bag
and	jam	Wag
hand	Sam	tag
land	am	rag
band	ram	bag
and	Sam	sag
sand	ham	rag
I	sēe	mē

Jan and Dan

I am Jan.
I can see Dan.
Dan can see me.

I am Dan.
I can see Jan.
Jan can see me.

Dan can see Wag.
Jan can see Wag.
Wag can see Dan and Jan.

Lesson 3

A a  ant

Practice sounding these words, listening for the short vowel sound. Say them until you know them.

căt	Dăd	băg
sat	had	tag
mat	Dad	Wag
hat	had	rag
sat	lad	sag
pat	mad	nag
mat	pad	wag
fat	bad	lag

the căt   the hăt   ĭs ĭn ŏn

4

A Cat in the Hat

I can see a hat.
Dad had the hat.
Wag can see the hat.

The hat is on the mat.
Wag sat on the mat.
Wag can pat the hat.

Wag can see a cat.
The cat can see Wag.
The cat is in the hat.

Lesson 4

A a

ant

| Dăd | năp | răn |
| lad | lap | can |

glad	cap	pan
Dad	tap	can
lad	map	ran

had	lap	man
sad	nap	ran
bad	tap	fan

to

Wag ran to Sam.

6

Wag and Sam

Wag had a nap.
Wag can see Sam.
Sam can see Wag.

Wag ran to Sam.
Sam ran to Wag.
Sam can tag Wag.
Wag is on Sam's lap.

I can see Wag on Sam's lap.
Wag is glad.
Sam is glad.

Lesson 5

A a  ant

| ănt | hăt | băg |
| and | pat | tag |

an	bag	fast
fan	Wag	last
ran	tag	past
pan	sag	cast

| not | | in |
| hot | | on |

An ant can work.

work   The ant is not on a mat.

8

Sam and the Ant

See the ant.
See the ant go fast.
Sam can see the ant.

The ant can go and go.
The ant can go in the bag.
See the ant go in the bag.

Sam can not see it in the bag.
The ant can work and work.
Sam can see the ant work.

Lesson 6

A a

ant

Practice sounding these words, listening for the short vowel sound. Say them until you know them.

căt	hănd	ăs
mat	hands	has
bat	will	bass
fat	bill	lass
mat	fill	mass
pat	hill	pass
(ŭ)		
Mother	hĕlp	fôr
Mother	help	for
to		
do		

Mother has work to do.
I can help Mother.

Sam and Jan Help

Mother has work to do.
Sam and Jan can work for Mother.
Dan will not help.

Mother is glad to see Jan help.
Mother is glad to see Sam help.
Mother is sad Dan will not work.

Mother will help Dan work.
Dan's hands will work for Mother.

Lesson 7

I i

insects

Practice sounding these words, listening for the short vowel sound. Say them until you know them.

lĭd	pĭg	wĭll
did	big	hill
hid	big	Jill
bid	wig	Bill
did	dig	will
rid	pig	still

dŏll   gift
doll   lift

Jill can lift the gift.

12

Jill and the Gift

Jill can see a gift.
The gift is big.
A lid is on the gift.

Jill will lift the lid.
Jill will see the gift.
The gift is a doll.

The doll sits still.
Jill will lift the doll.
Jill is glad for the doll.

Lesson 8

I i

insects

6

fĭsh	sĭck	sĭx
wish	Dick	fix
dish	pick	mix

shē		sĭt
wē	pizza	fit
mē		hit
hē	is	pit
bē	in	bit
	it	

Jill will help Miss Hill.

14

Jill Helps

Miss Hill is sick.
Miss Hill has to sit.

Jill will see Miss Hill.
She has a gift.

Jill will fix a pizza for Miss Hill.
The pizza is on a dish.
Miss Hill is glad.
Jill is glad, too.
We will be glad if we will help.

Lesson 9

I i

insects

Practice sounding these words, listening for the short vowel sound. Say them until you know them.

zĭp	crĭb	hit
rip	bib	fit
tip	rib	
		it
lip	this	bit
nip	kiss	kit
hip	miss	

hĭm		
Tim	rēad	She can read.
Kim		He can read.
dim		We can read.
	sĭt	

16

Pam and Bill

This is Pam and Bill.
Pam will sit.
Bill is in his crib.

Pam can help him.
She will read to him.
He will not tip if he is still.

Bill is glad.
He is glad if Pam will read.

Lesson 10

I i

insects

Practice sounding these words, listening for the short vowel sound. Say them until you know them.

ănt	Gŏd	dĭsh
plant		wish
	Jĭll	fish
pĭck	fill	
sick	bill	ĭt It
lick	hill	is Is
Dick	will	in In
tick	pill	if If
	is	sĭx
	his	fix
mādе		

God made the plants.

18

Work For Tim

Tim has to work.
He will help Mother.

Tim had to plant for Mother.
He will pick for his mother, too.

His mother will fix a big dish.
The dish will be for Tim.
It will be for Jill and Dick, too.

God made the plants.
God made the plants to be big.

Lesson 11

U u  umbrella

Practice sounding these words, listening for the short vowel sound. Say them until you know them.

jŭmp	Mŭff	stĭck
bump	cuff	pick
hump	puff	Dick
dump	huff	lick
pump		sick
	mŭst	
kĭss	dust	hĭt
miss	rust	fit

gĭve   Mother will give Jan a kiss.
thank   Jan will thank Mother.

Mother Will Help

Jan has a bump.
She hit a big stick.

Jan must sit.
Mother will help Jan.
Mother will fix the bump.

Mother will give Jan a kiss.
Jan will hug and kiss Mother.

Muff can see Mother and Jan.
Muff can see Jan thank Mother.

Lesson 12

U u  umbrella

bŭs   sŭn   pŭp

us   run   cup

fuss   fun   up

        gun

băck   bun   dŭst

sack   must

pack   făst   rust

rack   past   gust

tack   last   crust

        cast

The big bus will go fast.

The Bus

See the man.
See the bus, Pam.
The man has a big bus.

We must run to go on the bus.
Run, Pam, run.
I will run, too.

At last we can sit on the bus.
We must sit back.
It will go up a hill fast.
It is fun to go in the big bus.

Lesson 13
U u

umbrella

Practice sounding these words, listening for the short vowel sound. Say them until you know them.

bŭg	cŭp	lunch
mug	pup	bunch
hug	up	punch
rug		munch
	sun	
gŭm		dŭst
hum	ăsk	must
bum	task	rust
	mask	
bŭn		mĭlk
fun	gĭve	silk
	live	

Pam Helps Bill

Mother had to ask Pam to help.
The task is to help Bill.
Pam must give Bill his lunch.
The lunch is in the cup.

Pam has a mug, too.
Milk is in the mug.
It is fun to help Bill.
Bill is glad.
Pam is glad to help Mother and Bill.

Lesson 14

U u  umbrella

dŭck	swĭm	săck
tuck	him	back
buck	rim	rack
puck	Tim	quack
jŭmp	bŭd	ŭp
bump	mud	pup
dump	suds	cup

God made the duck.
God made the pup.
God made the pig.
God made everything.

26

Tim and Jill

Jill and Tim can see a duck.
It can quack and swim.
God made the duck.

Tim can see a pig.
The pig is glad to be in mud.
God made the pig.

Jill can see a pup.
It can run and jump.
God made the pup.

God made Tim and Jill.
God made everything we can see.